GETTING THE
MESSAGE

Film and Video

How to interpret
what we see, read and hear

Sean Connolly

W
FRANKLIN WATTS
Schools Library and Information Services

 An Appleseed Editions book

First published in 2009 by Franklin Watts
338 Euston Road, London NW1 3BH

Franklin Watts Australia
Hachette Children's Books
Level 17/207 Kent St, Sydney, NSW 2000

© 2009 Appleseed Editions

Created by Appleseed Editions Ltd,
Well House, Friars Hill, Guestling,
East Sussex TN35 4ET

Designed by Helen James
Edited by Mary-Jane Wilkins
Picture research by Su Alexander

ISBN 978 07496 8781 6

Dewey Classification: 302.23' 4

A CIP catalogue for this book is available from the British Library.

Photograph acknowledgements
page 6 Frank Trapper/Corbis; 8 & 11 Bettmann/Corbis; 12 Mitchell Gerber/Corbis;
15 Artisan Pics/The Kobal Collection; 16 Robert Landau/Corbis; 18 Martin H Simon/
Corbis; 21 Owen Franken/Corbis; 22 Andrew Cooper/Columbia/Spyglass/Bureau
L.A.Collection/Corbis; 24 DreamWorks Distribution LLC./Special Anti-Pesto Still
(Aardma/Bureau L.A. Collection/Corbis; 26 Reuters/Corbis; 29 Sherwin Crasto/
Reuters/Corbis; 30 Swim Inc 2, LLC/Corbis; 33 Austrian Archives/Corbis; 34 John
Springer Collection/Corbis; 37 New Line/The Kobal Collection/Nelson, Ralph JR;
38 David Bebber/Reuters/Corbis; 41 Ken Stepnell/Photolibrary; 42 Getty Images
Front cover Robert Landau/Corbis

Printed in China

Franklin Watts is a division of Hachette Children's Books,
an Hachette Livre UK company.
www.hachettelivre.co.uk

Contents

The power of pictures

'Every picture tells a story.'
'A picture is worth a thousand words.'
'The story paints a complete picture of his life.'

People are fascinated with pictures, as these familiar sayings demonstrate. Most human beings are limited to one of the world's 6000 languages, so they can find it hard to understand each other. Works of literature stand among the greatest artistic masterpieces, but the building blocks that make them great – words – can also act as barriers to those who do not speak the same language.

Pictures are another matter. They affect people immediately. No one can say for sure whether human beings developed

Some of the leading characters add excitement to the opening night (first screening) of Star Wars: Episode II *in Hollywood. New films can still capture the public's imagination – just as they did in the 1920s and 1930s.*

languages before they could draw, but cave paintings are our only link with ancestors who lived more than 30,000 years ago. Those early humans must have felt a magical power as they painted images of lions, wolves and each other on the walls of caves. By the flickering light of their campfires, these early artists recorded some sacred events for eternity.

Modern magic

This sense of magic continues to run through story-telling through pictures today. Modern story-telling uses film and video rather than paint on cave walls, but the results are surprisingly similar. During the two hours or so we spend in a darkened cinema, we allow ourselves to be transported to faraway places. We go on a journey mapped out by the film-maker, only returning to our own world when the lights go on again.

Experts describe how cinema audiences can put their trust in a film-maker by suspending their disbelief – choosing not to doubt that a hero can fly or that the beautiful princess will fall in love with the frog. The audience's feeling of being entertained depends on that willingness not to ask questions.

Great film-makers know exactly how to manipulate the way people think or see things. Their reputations are built on this magical skill. But this ability to manipulate people's thinking can also be a dangerous weapon. Some films 'rewrite history', twisting the truth about real events. Others try to influence the way people think about what they will buy or how they intend to vote. And evil people have tapped the enormous power of film to stir up hatred and fear – even to drive people to war. Like any kind of magic, films must be handled – and viewed – with care.

TALKING HEADS

'I think cinema, movies, and magic have always been closely associated. The very earliest people who made film were magicians.'

American film director Francis Ford Coppola

In the frame

Film-making is a modern art form, hardly more than a century old. It developed from the ancient tradition of drama – public performances of plays. That tradition fulfils one of people's most basic needs: to tell stories. Organized drama began thousands of years ago, when people gathered in naturally curving valleys, where actors' voices from a makeshift stage could reach audience members high above them.

The ancient Indians, Chinese and Greeks were writing and performing plays more than 2500 years ago. Europeans carried on the Greek tradition through the time of the Roman empire and beyond. Medieval Europeans used drama as a way of teaching illiterate people about religion and morality.

As the dramatic tradition continued into the early modern period, it joined with other art forms. Ballet grew out of dance and opera developed as a mixture of music and drama. Spoken drama in the form of plays also flourished with the works of William Shakespeare, the French dramatist Molière and the playwright Friedrich Schiller from Germany.

As many as 50,000 people watched battles between gladiators in the arenas of ancient Rome. The most successful gladiators were as popular as today's film stars.

A permanent revolution

No matter how varied these spectacles were, they shared one important characteristic – they were not permanent. Once the curtain fell on a play, ballet or opera, that performance was lost. No one would see that exact mixture of talking, moving, acting or singing again.

All this changed during the nineteenth century with the invention and development of motion pictures. The technical ability to take an accurate picture and record it on film was the first step. Then inventors found ways of taking a sequence of filmed pictures and projecting them on a screen to give the effect of movement.

Inventors in several countries came up with similar ideas simultaneously to create 'moving photography' at the end of the century. But it took a pair of French brothers – Auguste and Louis Lumière – to see the real potential of this new invention. On 28 December 1895, they showed ten short films in the basement of a café in Paris. Although the performance was no longer than 20 minutes, it was the first public screening of motion pictures. Cinema as we know it was born.

A new industry

One of the films screened by the Lumière brothers showed a train arriving at a station. Modern audiences might find the sequence a bit clumsy, or even funny, but nineteenth-century audiences had never seen anything like it. Some people were terrified and fled from the café. Others stayed for more thrills. That single event, highlighting people's desire to be entertained and even scared, showed the future of cinema.

An industry soon grew out of this new form of entertainment. Film-makers saw that this new medium could provide both rousing amusement and artistic expression. Just as importantly, business people saw that audiences were eager for more and more of it.

SPOTLIGHT ON
How film works

At its heart, film relies on illusion. When an audience leaves the cinema at the end of a film, they have not seen anything which actually moves. Instead they have seen about 170,000 still photographs shown in quick succession. Film runs through the projector at the rate of 24 separate photographs (called frames) per second. Instead of seeing all these photographs as a speeded-up slideshow, the brain sees free-flowing movement from start to finish. That is because of an experience known as the persistence of vision. Our brains hold on to an image that our eyes see for a bit longer than we actually see it. When the eye sees images at a very fast rate – such as 24 per second, as in a film – it connects the separate images and makes them flow together.

Developing a system of producing sounds to accompany the images on a movie screen took more than 30 years. These were the decades of the silent film, and motion pictures told their stories through the silent actions of the cast, helped now and then by intertitles that moved the story along.

Two major breakthroughs led to the development of films as we know them. In the late 1920s, films became 'talkies' – they were no longer silent. And about ten years later, the first colour films were produced. In the twenty-first century cinemas still show films that were produced with techniques used during the late 1930s.

The big difference between now and then is that films have to compete for our attention with television, DVDs and the Internet. Film-makers can no longer take it for granted that people will flock to every new film. But in their quest to produce something louder, funnier, scarier or more romantic, they continue to try to summon up some magic.

Opposite: Charlie Chaplin directed and starred in some of the most famous films of the silent era. Many of his films, such as Modern Times *(right), poked fun at the way people lived in the modern world.*

WIDE OF THE MARK

'Our invention can be exploited for a certain time as a scientific curiosity, but apart from that, it has no commercial future whatsoever.'

Auguste Lumière, on the impact of the first public cinema performance.

THE POWER OF SILENCE

CAN YOU THINK OF WAYS IN WHICH SILENT FILMS WERE BETTER THAN TODAY'S FILMS OR DO YOU THINK THAT MODERN TECHNIQUES HAVE LED TO IMPROVEMENTS IN EVERY WAY?

Over to YOU

Lights! Camera! Action!

You can imagine with ease how difficult it is to produce the *Lord of the Rings* or *Star Wars* films. These motion pictures take years to complete and rely on huge sets, large casts and complicated special effects. How do film-goers know that these films are the result of such painstaking efforts? The evidence is in the exciting battle sequences and the way these films bring to life worlds that would otherwise remain in someone's imagination.

SPOTLIGHT ON
Film stages

Most films, no matter how large or small their budget, go through similar stages before they appear on screens. A fraction of the overall budget is devoted to each stage; dividing the spending like this makes it easier to see whether – and where – too much money is being spent.

The first stage, known as development, covers the stages from the initial idea of the film through to a script. This script becomes the first working draft of the film. Using the script as a guide, the film company hires the cast and crew for the next stage – pre-production. This is also the time when the filming schedule is worked out; stages are hired or built and locations are chosen according to this schedule.

Production is the stage that is familiar to most outsiders. This is the 'Lights! Camera! Action!' stage. During this time, the basic elements of the film (mainly the acting) are recorded. Filming is over at the end of this stage – unless scenes need to be reshot – but the film is usually much longer than it will be when it is shown.

The next stage, known as post-production, can be complicated and last far longer than production. This is when the film is edited, and music and special effects added. Even films that seem lifelike and natural need to be reworked carefully during this stage so that the finished product does not seem jumpy because of the editing. Once post-production is complete, the film can be released (see pages 18-19).

Opposite: director Sydney Pollack (left) and leading actor Harrison Ford discuss a scene as they work on location in New York City making the 1995 film Sabrina.

However, films and the film industry can be deceptive. A film that is set in the real world – a Welsh village, a New York neighbourhood or a Brazilian prison for example – might seem far easier to produce than a sci-fi blockbuster. If the story and characters are believable, audiences often imagine that shooting the film was simply a matter of keeping the camera in focus and not running out of film.

Teamwork and surprises

The truth is that every type of film – no matter how long or dependent on special effects – relies on teamwork from start to finish. In fact, it is often harder to produce a true-to-life scene than it is to depict a warrior's battle with a vicious dragon or space monster. That is because, at its heart, cinema is all about illusion.

A director often chooses not to shoot a film in the right order. For example, he or she might choose to film all the outdoor scenes in one go because the weather may change. Or if one or more of the main stars is only available for part of the schedule, all his or her scenes may be shot in a batch. No matter what choices were made in the production stage about shooting scenes, the director, editor and other key players will often rework the film in post-production (see previous page). After all, the finished product is simply a series of individual photographs and the order of those photographs can be changed.

Choosing video

Editing a film to create the exact story that the director wants is rewarding, but also time-consuming and expensive. And in order to be able to choose exactly which bits of film should be included, the director needs to shoot at least three times more film than will be seen on the screen. Simply buying enough film to shoot six hours of action (three times the length of a typical film) costs a lot of money.

Many new directors, who have little money to spend, choose to shoot their films with video equipment. Using their own cameras and video cassettes, they can shoot sequences, see them immediately, reshoot if necessary and then edit the whole thing on their computers. The savings are enormous, and many directors would never have succeeded if they had not been able to break into the industry via video.

However, even the best videos lack the sharp visual quality of film, so directors hope to move on from video once they have established themselves. Occasionally, though, the limitations of video can turn out to be surprising advantages (see Talking Heads).

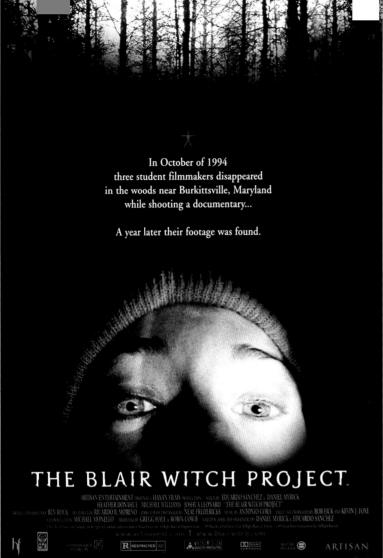

The makers of The Blair Witch Project *had little money to publicize their film, but news about it spread quickly through the Internet.*

A LOW-BUDGET SUCCESS STORY

In 1998, Eduardo Sanchez and Daniel Myrick directed a low-budget horror film called *The Blair Witch Project.* Their lack of money actually helped to make the film (about a video documentary that was lost in a haunted wood) more believable. Sanchez recalls some of the commercial rules they broke on their way to a worldwide success. 'We started to realize that every weakness of independent film, we could use to our advantage. We couldn't have any stars. We shot it all on video. We didn't need lighting. We had just one location, for the most part.'

A key to the credits

Next time you go to the cinema, stay and watch all the credits at the end of the film. They roll up the screen for several minutes, giving a clear idea of just how many people are involved in producing a film. Some of the job titles – such as director, producer and editor – are easy to understand. Others, including key grip, best boy and gaffer, tell us that the world of film has a language all its own.

Film-making requires far more equipment than the lights (left) and camera shown here.

On the next page are some of the jobs that appear on film credits, and a brief description of each. Remember this list is not complete although it does give an idea of the variety of people involved.

Art director is in charge of the artists and craftsmen who build the sets.

Assistant director keeps track of the shooting schedule of a film and how it is progressing.

Best boy is the main assistant to either the gaffer or the key grip.

Cinematographer (also called director of photography) helps to give the film the look the director wants by guiding the camera operators and set designers.

Director is in charge of all the creative aspects of a film, from the hiring of actors through the shooting and all stages of production.

Dolly grip sets up the dolly (a wheeled track which allows the camera to roll smoothly).

Foley artist creates dramatic sound effects (thuds, bangs and cracks) to be added to the film to make it more dramatic.

Gaffer sets up the lighting on a film set.

Key grip is in charge of setting up equipment so the camera crew can get the right shots.

Location manager finds locations (places where a film can be shot outside a studio) and obtains permission to film there.

Producer is in charge of the business side of a film at every stage of its making and distribution.

Screenwriter prepares an existing work (such as a novel or play) or writes a new story to form the basis of a film.

Over
to
YOU

IMPORTANT DIRECTORS

SOME FILM DIRECTORS ARE CALLED *AUTEURS* (FRENCH FOR AUTHORS) BECAUSE THEY HAVE SO MUCH INFLUENCE OVER THE FINISHED PRODUCT. AUDIENCES AND CRITICS EXPECT A CERTAIN LOOK AND FEEL TO THEIR FILMS THAT NO ONE ELSE CAN MATCH. DO YOU THINK THAT ANY SINGLE PERSON SHOULD BE SO MUCH MORE IMPORTANT THAN THE OTHER CREATIVE PEOPLE WHO HELP MAKE A FILM?

General release

The global film industry is worth hundreds of billions of pounds each year. There is huge competition to have films distributed and to share in this huge payout, so the money men have enormous influence. Long after the creatives (the director, cast, writers and composers) have done their work, it is the responsibility of the business people to show a film on as many screens as possible.

The money experts consider a film as a product, like a car or a refrigerator, which needs to be sold skilfully. And if people are slow to accept the product, they will often ask directors to change a film – just as sweet-makers change their goods to try to sell more of them. Films are often cut – so audiences will not find them long or dull – and even the ending of a film could be reshot because of audience reaction at a test screening.

Many people prefer to watch films in their own homes rather than the cinema. Viewers can take out and return DVDs at 24-hour booths, like the one shown here in Washington DC.

Once the film company decides a film is ready, it works out a deal with a film distributor to show it in as many cinemas as possible. This wide distribution of the film is called general release. The distributor looks after every stage of getting a film shown – dealing with individual cinemas, chains of cinemas, television companies (for eventual TV screenings) and stores to sell DVDs and other copies of the film.

The bottom line

Using this traditional commercial system, a great deal of money has to be spent on a film before it can earn money back. The American film industry, based in the Los Angeles district of Hollywood, developed along these business lines. Big film companies, known as studios, produced most American films for decades. And although there are fewer Hollywood studios than in the 1940s, these companies still have a great deal of influence.

Big studios have always considered the bottom line closely. This is the amount of money a film eventually makes or loses once it is shown. They find it easier to produce films that fall within some traditional genres, such as comedies, thrillers, chick flicks (films aimed at women), horror films and so on. And a typical studio film also follows some unwritten rules about how it treats its characters. Alfred Hitchcock's 1960 film *Psycho* broke one of the main studio rules because its lead character was killed just a third of the way through the film. Hitchcock was already a famous and successful director: a newcomer would never have received studio funding for such a film.

More choice?

Multi-screen cinemas have been around for 50 years or more, but until the 1990s most had only two or three screens. Since then, a new type of multi-screen cinema has become common, called the multiplex. A multiplex has up to 16 screens, offering a wide choice of film to audiences in a particular area. Many multiplexes are on the outskirts of towns and cities, so audiences have to drive there.

Supporters of multiplexes claim that these huge cinemas – which are often linked to bars and restaurants – have helped to keep the film industry alive. Films face threats from all sides, including competition from downloaded films, DVDs and other forms of entertainment. But critics point out that every multiplex in a country seems to show the same films. Also, these giant super-cinemas have the power to drive smaller, independent cinemas out of business, just as out-of-town supermarkets have damaged the businesses of smaller shopkeepers in towns.

Influential big companies can negotiate tough business deals for their films. They also find it easier than smaller companies and film-makers to promote films through marketing tie-ins, such as free film superheroes inside boxes of cereal.

TALKING HEADS

FAILING THE TESTS

Director Steven Spielberg's experiences as a film-maker have made him a strong critic of test screenings. 'I just found that the test screenings for *Hook, Always, The Color Purple* and *Empire of the Sun* didn't teach me anything. In fact, it got me to cut things out to please the audience that I wouldn't normally cut out. An audience might respond negatively on a Wednesday night, so you'd make all these changes, but you could take that same film and show it to a different audience on the following Friday and get a positive reaction.'

SPOTLIGHT ON
Indie films

Some films reach cinemas without going through the studio system. These independent, or indie, films usually have smaller budgets and their makers find it harder to reach the widest audiences. On the other hand, they are not forced to follow the rigid guidelines that studios impose, so they can tell their stories in unusual and sometimes unexpected ways.

Recently, independent film-makers have used the Internet successfully rather than approaching studios. Many films now earn their reputation through word of mouth, echoed again and again on social network websites. A buzz created on the Internet can lead to a screening at a film festival; that publicity in turn can provide a real boost for a relatively low-budget indie film.

The French city of Cannes holds a major film festival every year in May;
film-makers use such festivals to build publicity for their latest features.

Over to YOU

NOT MY TYPE

FOR DECADES, FILM-MAKERS AND AUDIENCES DESCRIBED EVERY FILM AS BELONGING TO A PARTICULAR TYPE (OR GENRE AS PEOPLE IN THE FILM INDUSTRY SAY). IT MIGHT BE A WESTERN, A ROMANTIC COMEDY, A MYSTERY OR A WAR FILM. SOME CRITICS BELIEVE THAT THE BEST MODERN FILMS DO NOT BELONG TO A SINGLE GENRE – THEY ARE OFTEN MIXTURES OF TWO OR MORE. DO YOU AGREE? AND IF SO, CAN YOU THINK OF ANY EXAMPLES – AND WHICH GENRES THEY COMBINE?

Reading a film

Most people leave the cinema with a clear idea of whether they have enjoyed the film they have just seen. But if asked why they liked a particular film, they usually come up with rather simple answers, such as: 'it was really funny', 'the special effects were cool', 'the ending was terribly sad' and so on.

Although they may not realize it, people making these judgements are paying much deeper compliments about the making of the film. Like a puppet show during which the audience ignores the strings, a good film hides many of the elements that make it work so well. Looking more closely and finding those elements can be rewarding.

Film lovers compare the portrayal of favourite characters in different films. The Legend of Zorro (above) features the famous masked hero who was first shown in silent film.

The funny bits may have succeeded because the actors and director worked to get the timing just right – sometimes doing scenes over and over or editing them to get just the right laugh. The special effects might have been impressive, but the way the director mixed them with real-life scenes made them fit into the film better. A sad ending is all the more powerful for having the right mixture of shots, music… and even silence.

Noticing these elements is sometimes called reading a film. And just as reading words can sometimes reveal surprises and even hidden messages, reading a film can lead to some surprising conclusions.

Learning to read

People studying literature learn that they can get more out of a novel or poem by reading it closely, or rereading it. The artistic force of a work becomes clearer when the reader can appreciate some of the techniques used by an author or poet. Close reading makes people ask questions, such as:
• Who is narrating this story?
• Do readers learn anything that the main character doesn't know?
• Is the story told through description or through dialogue?

Films are surprisingly similar. People may view them as two hours' worth of escapism – just as they might make snap judgements about what they read. But, just like written literature, films can be read and analysed more closely. Hundreds of books have been written about getting the most from films, but the key is to focus on two main areas: language and message.

Building a picture

The two sorts of reading – of books or of films – are very similar. Each builds on the basics below:
• A frame, one of the thousands of still images in a film, is like a letter – the basic building block.

• A single continuous shot is made up of frames in the same way that a word is made up of letters.

• A scene groups related shots together just as a sentence groups words.

• More complex still is a film sequence, which groups scenes together in the same way as an author groups sentences together to create a paragraph.

All films are made up of these elements, although the director may use them in unusual ways. Rather than being swept away by a film's story, someone analysing the film will probably ask similar questions to those questions listed above. These questions touch on a number of choices that the director makes, many of them to do with where the camera goes and what it shows (because that is what appears on the cinema screen).

Creators of animated films such as the Wallace and Gromit film The Curse of the Were-Rabbit *(left) work slowly and patiently, assembling their films frame by frame.*

Some questions about films might be:
• Does the camera leave the main character, or do we see only what he or she sees?
• Does dialogue at the beginning of the film provide clues about what happens later on?
• Does the music set a particular mood that helps us understand the film better?

Using these tools to appreciate films can be very effective. Most newspapers, as well as television stations and major websites, offer reviews of new films. The people who do this work – film reviewers – judge new films and express their views in an interesting and helpful way. Some film reviewers develop an international reputation; others are very young but still have their reviews published (see page 40).

TALKING HEADS

OUTSIDE AND IN

Vittorio Soraro is an Italian cinematographer who has worked with some of the world's most famous directors. Like him, they look at a film's story from the outside – it unfolds through the action and setting. Soraro, however, worked on the film *Reds* with American director Warren Beatty. Unlike most other directors, Beatty was also an actor, who saw the story developing from the inside – because that is how he understood it as an actor.

Soraro found this difference troubling at first, but then found ways of filming the story using both techniques: 'For me, in the European culture, the camera is its own character – it's the way that you are writing. So I decided to go inside, tried to see from the characters' point of view. And it was a great revelation. I discovered a world I didn't know. It gave me an incredible balance, to see the same sequence from outside and inside, from the characters' point of view or from a director's or a cinematographer's point of view.'

World cinema

The Lumière brothers may have dismissed the idea of a film industry (see page 11), but others were quick to see the business potential of film. After its informal birth in Paris in 1895, the film industry soon became linked to the United States and to the Los Angeles district of Hollywood in particular.

Director Ang Lee stands by a large-scale model of one of the four Academy Awards (the top Hollywood honour) he received in 2000 for the Chinese action film Crouching Tiger, Hidden Dragon.

In many ways, Hollywood is an ideal location for making films. The weather is usually sunny, making it easier to complete films without problems with the weather. At that time land in that part of Los Angeles was still cheap, making it possible to build large film studios. Taxes in California and the United States were low.

Film studios grew up in Hollywood, often headed by men who had long experience in other forms of entertainment. The industry was young and did not have the traditions and customs that make it hard for newcomers to enter, so many immigrants to the United States were able to set up and run new film studios. There was another surprising bonus: unlike other forms of entertainment, where these men struggled with English that might not be fluent, films were silent!

A global empire

The success of Hollywood, which continues into the twenty-first century, comes at a cost. The big film-making companies view their activity as a business rather than as a risk-taking form of entertainment. They often prefer to put their money in a few expensive films which they hope will earn them back even more money. As a result, fewer films are made, because the studio money has been spent on making and promoting the blockbusters.

Independent film-makers in the United States (see page 20) also suffer because the studios use their power to book all the screens at many cinemas. The indie film-makers have to rely on smaller independent cinemas to show their films.

Similarly, some countries have seen their entire film industries fade under the influence of the big Hollywood films, which are exported around the world. The top ten films in the UK are usually the same top ten as in the United States – and they are nearly all American films. France, Spain and Italy still produce films for home and abroad, but Hollywood also dominates their cinema screens.

SPOTLIGHT ON
Bollywood

The country that leads the world in the number of films produced – and cinema tickets sold – each year is not the United States. Despite the international distribution of American films and the enormous sums Hollywood blockbusters earn, the American film industry no longer leads the way in these important categories.

That honour goes to India, which has had a thriving film industry since the earliest years of cinema. The first Indian commercial cinemas opened in 1900, and a local industry soon developed to keep audiences supplied with all sorts of film.

This industry had strong ties with Great Britain (India was still part of the British Empire), but it continued to develop after India became independent in 1947.

The centre of this industry has always been Mumbai (until recently known as Bombay). People have nicknamed this Indian cinema heart Bollywood – a combination of Bombay and Hollywood. Most of the films produced there are in Hindi, the most widely spoken of the many languages in India. With India's huge population eager for entertainment, the film industry was able to grow simply by catering to this home market. Traditional Bollywood films contain lots of singing and dancing, and the set pieces are dramatic.

Bollywood films are becoming more and more popular outside India: Indian films are regularly screened around the world and several non-Indian directors (such as Australia's Baz Luhrmann) have given their films a lively Bollywood feel.

Some people outside the United States resent the crushing power of the American film industry, comparing it to the colonialism that European powers practised in previous centuries. Others take the view that business is business, and that 'if you can't beat them, join them'. Some of the most popular British films of recent years, such as *Bridget Jones' Diary* and the Harry Potter films, were made in Britain, but the money to fund them was American.

Opposite: Bollywood stars Rima Sen, Sunil Shetty and Gauhar Khan prepare for a dance sequence during the making of Aan (Men at Work) *in a major Mumbai film studio.*

ANCIENT CULTURE

Many people have been surprised by the enormous popularity of Bollywood. Suddenly the world has noticed what India has loved all along. And some people outside India believe that Bollywood has had to change itself in order to appeal to people in the rest of the world. But one of India's best-known films stars, Amitabh Bachchan, believes that Indian film-makers have never had to worry about what others think: 'Our culture hasn't changed for 5000 years... our stories never drive away from our basic ethos. There will always be the family union, the mother-son relationship, festivals, sacrifice, stories that are drawn ultimately from our mythology and our religion. We have everything laid out for us, we don't need to go looking elsewhere.'

Film as a weapon

Many legends and fairy tales centre on the clash between good and evil magic, with the opposing forces constantly trying to beat one another. In the film *The Wizard of Oz* the Good Witch of the North helps the heroine Dorothy in her struggle with the Evil Witch of the West. The seven *Harry Potter* novels (and five films) also depend on dramatic battles between good and bad magic.

Powerful battles between good and evil are not simply an exciting part of a film – sometimes the film itself is part of this battle. Since the birth of film, people have viewed it as a sort of magic, whether it was the Lumière brothers' train threatening to steam out of the screen or the death-defying antics of silent comedians such as Charlie Chaplin and Buster Keaton. Audiences have always been drawn into the world created by the director, actors and others who helped make the film.

Taking aim

During the early decades of the twentieth century there was enormous tension and turmoil in the world: new political systems (communism and fascism) threatened the democratic way of life in Europe and beyond. This rising conflict led to the Second World War and then a decades-long stand-off between the United States (and its allies) and the Soviet Union (and other communist nations) called the cold war. Fascism and communism represented unbending rules and a lack of individual freedom, but both used a form of popular entertainment – the cinema – as a tool to gain support, to rewrite history and to criticize people who opposed the government. Films became propaganda weapons.

The Russian film *The Battleship Potemkin* was made in 1925, just eight years after Russian communists seized power. The film depicted the rebellion of 1905 in which ordinary people were cruelly attacked by the forces of the tsar. The director, Sergei Eisenstein, wanted to emphasize the cruelty of the tsar's government. He wanted to contrast that behaviour with the innocence and decency of the people who protested (and who, according to the film, would later support the communists).

Nine years later, when Adolf Hitler and his Nazi party ruled Germany, Leni Riefenstahl made the film *Triumph of the Will*. The film was intended to be a record of the Nazi party convention in the city of Nuremberg, but it came to represent much more. Riefenstahl, like Eisenstein, knew exactly how to use the images on the screen to influence the way audiences thought. Even today, people seeing

Opposite: even the posters for the Russian film The Battleship Potemkin *were works of art, offering a clue about how unsettling the film itself would be.*

31

SPOTLIGHT ON
The Battleship Potemkin

Sergei Eisenstein developed the technique of montage to produce extremely dramatic effects in his films. In the most famous scene from *The Battleship Potemkin*, the tsar's troops march on protesters who have gathered on a large outside staircase. The audience sees quick shots of different actions in quick succession, with the camera returning briefly to some of them and lingering on others.

• A mother holding a sick child appeals to the soldiers.

• A man wearing glasses cries out.

• Another woman is pushing a pram.

• The first woman is shot.

• The man's glasses are on the ground – with a bullet hole in one lens.

• Troops march across the bodies of the first woman and her child.

• People begin to panic.

• The soldiers continue their march down the steps.

• The woman with the pram stands between the soldiers and her baby.

• The soldiers continue to march.

• The woman screams and is shot.

• She falls back against the pram, sending it down the steps – slowly at first, then faster – with the baby still inside it.

Each of these images lasts no more than a few seconds, and shots of the pram (moving faster and faster) continue to be mixed with the scenes showing crowds, soldiers and weapons. The effect is overwhelming: few people watching the film could feel any sympathy for the evil soldiers. Audiences leave the film believing that everything that the tsar stood for was cruel and designed to crush ordinary people – thank goodness the communists took over. No one could really believe there was another side to the story – and that is how Eisenstein wanted it.

the film for the first time are astounded at how the director has taken something we consider to be dull and boring – a big political meeting – and turned it into a spectacular event. And the leader who is now considered to be one of the most evil people in history – Adolf Hitler – is shown to be like an ancient hero, as his plane breaks through the clouds on his way to address thousands of adoring supporters.

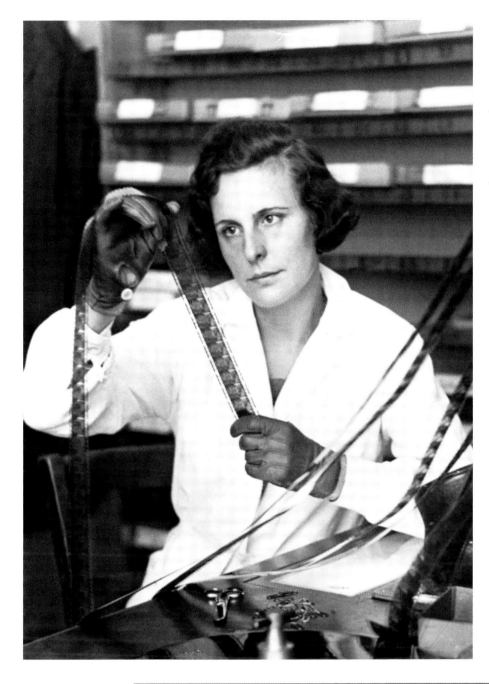

Leni Riefenstahl examined her films frame by frame during the editing process, making sure that every second of the finished film was exactly as she wanted it to appear on the screen.

Over to YOU

OUTLAWED?

IT WAS ILLEGAL TO SHOW *THE BATTLESHIP POTEMKIN* IN BRITISH CINEMAS FOR SEVERAL DECADES BECAUSE THE GOVERNMENT BELIEVED THAT IT WOULD ENCOURAGE REVOLUTION IN BRITAIN. CAN YOU THINK WHY THIS MIGHT HAVE BEEN A BAD DECISION? A GOOD ONE?

Does the camera lie?

It is easy to detect the propaganda in films set in the First or Second World Wars. Major events, and the works involved with them, make more sense when time has passed. And the reasons for resorting to propaganda also become a little clearer to us.

For example, we now know that, during the first years of the Second World War, the British government was keen to put pressure on the United States (which was still neutral) to join the war against Nazi Germany. The government lent support to film-makers shooting motion pictures about the British standing together through thick and thin, about the evils of the

Many British films made during the Second World War, such as Mrs Minniver *(left), showed a 'never say die' spirit in the face of bombing. Such films helped to boost spirits and also persuaded many Americans to support Britain in the war.*

Nazi government and about the bravery of those in the British armed services. Many films produced during that time might have seemed like love stories or action tales, but at their heart they were pleading with America to join the fight.

Does this mean that the Allies were no better than the Nazis because they also used propaganda when making their films? And what about today – are modern cinema audiences still influenced by hidden messages in films?

Looking more closely

It is harder to judge current films to see whether they might contain propaganda messages. Even when some viewers decide that current events or historical details are distorted in a particular film, others will come to its defence. And occasionally, former allies have opposing views about how a story should be told. Audiences in Britain, Canada and Australia often come out of Hollywood films thinking, 'Oh – so the Yanks think they won the Second World War by themselves.'

The United States government has no direct control over the film industry, but some people believe that the most powerful film centre in the world (Hollywood) acts on its behalf. Hollywood films, because they are shown so widely, can shape people's opinions about the role of the United States – and its relations with other countries.

Two recent American presidents – Ronald Reagan in the 1980s and George W. Bush since 2001 – have described America's enemies as evil. And some Hollywood films have echoed this view. *Behind Enemy Lines* (made in 2001) depicted the Serbs as bloodthirsty killers. At the time, US soldiers were fighting Serbs. *Black Hawk Down* (2002) was set in the East African nation of Somalia: the Muslim Somali fighters seem untrustworthy and shadowy compared with the more rounded portrayals of American soldiers.

SPOTLIGHT ON
Product placement

The messages hidden in films are not limited to patriotism. Companies have long been aware that having their products displayed in a popular film is an ideal form of advertising – especially since it is not true advertising, so viewers are watching closely. Film studios know that companies will pay to have their products shown in this way. The makers of the James Bond film *Casino Royale*, for example, made deals with the manufacturers of expensive wristwatches, vodka, computers, mobile phones and cars. This type of subtle advertising is called product placement, because the product is placed in a highly visible position. So when a handsome hero or gorgeous heroine needs to know the time, order a drink at a bar or drive up to a posh hotel, he or she will use one of the products that the film studio has been paid to include in the film.

Some companies have developed to act as links between manufacturers and film companies. One London-based company, just 20 years old, secures product placement in about 100 films each year. A look at its website shows the logos of companies that have used its services. The products represented include cars, peanuts, beers, computers and even nappies.

TALKING HEADS

CARS ON DISPLAY

BMW representatives are open about the importance of product placement, as this statement points out: 'Having its cars placed in a variety of films, television plays and documentaries benefits BMW in many ways. Global publicity, communicated in part by subliminal means and partly by overt ones, is positive and important, because it reaches a wide section of the public quite often on a world-wide scale and, with repeats, this can even become an audience of several millions.'

Some modern American films such as Pleasantville (left) poke fun at earlier films that suggested that people can find happiness in small towns where everyone thinks the same way and lives in identical houses.

People even see a sort of propaganda in historical romances such as *Pearl Harbor* (made in 2001 about the events that drove America into the Second World War 60 years before). Many young Americans only know about the historical events of 1941 through the story of this film, which portrays the Japanese as heartless robots.

Viewing society

Films often reinforce views that are common during a particular time or place. In many countries, for example, the 1980s was a decade of fierce business competition and patriotism. For some it had been a troubling time of unemployment and political scandal: films from the 1970s reflected that mood as well. But can we see this when we are in the middle of such periods ourselves? And would it affect how we saw and appreciated a film if we could read these themes within it?

Over to YOU

TV VERSUS FILM

MANY COUNTRIES IMPOSE STRICT LIMITS ON PRODUCT PLACEMENT AND OTHER TYPES OF HIDDEN MESSAGES GOING INTO TELEVISION PROGRAMMES, BUT NOT INTO FILMS. DO YOU THINK RULES SHOULD BE STRICTER FOR FILMS? OR LESS STRICT FOR TELEVISION?

Coming attractions

Young people have loved films for as long as film has existed. Generations of people have enjoyed settling down comfortably in a cinema, waiting for the lights to go down and the film to begin. Many of the best comedies, westerns and action films have been aimed at children. Some types of film – especially blockbusters such as the *Star Wars* and *Harry Potter* films – have been made almost exclusively for children.

Since the 1950s, children have been able to watch films in different settings. Many favourite family films, such as *The Sound of Music* and *The Great Escape,* have remained popular because they have been shown regularly on television. Being able to watch and record videos and DVDs has made it even easier for young people to watch all sorts of films. And technology continues to advance, offering new ways of watching films (see pages 42-43).

DIY films

The big difference between the present and even the recent past is how easy it is for anyone – including young people – to become involved with films and film-making. A great way to learn anything is by doing it, and by using trial and error methods when instruction is not available. And with the opportunity and technical means to do just that, young people are taking their first steps towards proper film-making.

Opposite: Daniel Radcliffe, star of the enormously popular Harry Potter *films, has made the transition from child star to respected dramatic actor.*

The route that most take into film-making today is through videos (see page 14). Most of today's mobile phones contain movie-making features, so that anyone can try to become a film director or actor. This do-it-yourself film industry has been one of the driving forces behind the way that the Internet has developed. Video-sharing websites such as YouTube have allowed users to contribute to the web rather than just watch it.

Going for guidance

Advances in technology have gone beyond simply offering people the technology to shoot their own films. It is now possible to come up with a film idea and take it through nearly every stage of production (see page 13). New software packages allow home-made films to be edited on computers and laptops. That means that a learner director can come up with a finished product that looks far better than previously.

SPOTLIGHT ON
Little Big Shots

Young people in Australia are lucky to be able to become involved with Little Big Shots, an international film festival that tours the country. This festival is special because all of the films are about, for, or even made by children.

Children are encouraged to write reviews of the films they watch, and to enter these reviews in a competition. The ten winners, some as young as six, take a three-day holiday from school to go on a film-making course at the Australian Centre for the Moving Image in Melbourne. To help budding reviewers start out, the Little Big Shots website offers five helpful tips, along the lines of those below:

• Remember the different elements that go into making a film. Pick out a few of these and say whether or not you think they work.

• Explain a bit about the plot but don't give away too much (especially any surprising twists).

• Imagine that you are reading the review, so write with interest – and don't begin by saying 'this film is about'.

• Tell the readers what you thought about the stars and their performances.

• How did the film make you feel, and did those feelings change while you were watching the film?

But having all the right tools does not automatically make anyone a real film-maker. If that were true, then anyone with a computer – or even a pencil and paper – could become a published writer. And as with writing, or art, or music, people still benefit from learning the basics from experienced instructors.

Through school and beyond, people can become involved in film studies, a broad subject that includes learning how to read films (see pages 22-25) as much as how to set about making them. Many schools have film clubs which tie in with these aims; likewise young people can turn to dozens of organizations to learn about films, share ideas and set about making films of their own. Even if local schools or youth

clubs have no film-making activities, young people can still become involved in theatre. Skills learned on the stage – acting or as part of the crew – are a good introduction to similar activities in film-making.

Film-making has always had a big presence on the Internet: many websites concentrate on involving young people with the whole film process (see page 45). And the Internet can instantly display finished products – either for study or to showcase work – so this is often the best way to pick up ideas.

There is no single way of becoming a film director. But whether a director learned the craft through reading about it, taking on odd jobs in a film company or simply by watching lots of films as a child, the training helps in later life. And in later years the world can look back on some of the director's first efforts as previews of coming attractions.

The Australian Centre for the Moving Image in Melbourne.

What's in store?

Films have been around for just over a century, and in that time the industry has made great leaps forward while holding on to the mystery that still attracts people to the cinema. Some advances, such as developing sound techniques and moving from black and white films to colour, have paved the way for the future. Others, such as 3D films and the 1960s Smell-O-Vision (bringing smells into a cinema) were failures.

Developments in other areas of communications, such as television, the Internet and mobile telephones, have sometimes threatened the future of films. During the 1950s, for example, many experts believed

SPOTLIGHT ON
3D cinema

A cinema screen is flat, so the images projected on to it can only appear in two dimensions – height and width. For many years film-makers have tried to present films that appear to have three dimensions (3D) – height, width and depth. Adding that third dimension, depth, would make films much more realistic.

Some films in the 1950s were advertised as being 3D, and audiences wore special cardboard spectacles to see the effects on the screen. But the effects were patchy and unrealistic, and for decades people joked about what a bad idea 3D films were.

Cinema audiences might be thinking differently by 2010. Several types of revolutionary new technology could allow audiences to see images that seem to be fully formed. One of these techniques combines the traditional film-making techniques of acting with video-game technology. The result will be a film in which the audience can view the action from any angle, and not just the traditional face-on front view.

Opposite: young people familiar with interactive video games (left) will soon be able to have a hands-on experience watching films in the cinema.

that having televisions in nearly every home would spell the end of cinemas. People would not want to go out and pay to see a film when they could stay at home watching television programmes.

Films soon regained their popularity when people realized that having a laugh at a film comedy – or even a scream at a horror film – was much more fun with other people, and not shut away from the rest of the world. Computer and telephone technology might seem to threaten film-making in the same way today, but films will probably coexist with these technologies in the future. After all, films are shown regularly on television, and DVDs and pay-per-view also use television to show films that have already been shown in cinemas. The magic of that experience – the large screen, the darkened room, the popcorn, the hushed murmurs of excitement – looks likely to take film and video well into its second century and beyond.

Glossary

allies Countries that join forces during a war.

blockbuster An extremely successful film, often – but not always –expensive to make.

cast The actors who take part in a film.

communism A political system in which all property is owned by the community and each person contributes and receives according to their ability and needs. A communist government provides work, health care, education and housing, but may deny people certain freedoms.

crew The team of people, other than the cast, which works on a film.

dialogue The words spoken by actors in a film.

ethos A guiding principle.

fascism A political system that includes belief in the supremacy of one national or ethnic group and contempt for democracy, and insists on obedience to a powerful leader.

film festival A gathering of film-makers and film-lovers, at which films are shown.

frame A single film image (24 of which are shown per second in a film).

genre A category of film or novel, such as love story, western, horror story, etc.

intertitle Words on a screen in a silent film, giving information about the action.

location A place away from a studio where filming is done.

medieval Concerning the Middle Ages, from roughly AD 500 to 1500.

medium One of the media, or different forms of mass communication, including print, radio and television.

montage A film technique that uses a series of different images in quick succession.

Nazi The name of the fascist party which governed Germany just before and during the Second World War.

neutral Not taking part in a war.

patriotism Vigorous support for your own country.

projector The bright lamp that shines film images on a screen.

propaganda Information intended to make people think in a certain way, sometimes ignoring or mocking other points of view.

Roman empire The vast area of Europe, Africa and Asia controlled by Rome from about 100 BC to AD 45.

Second World War The war from 1939-1945 between Germany, Japan, Italy and their allies against the UK, United States, China and their allies.

scene   A short section of a film that takes place in a particular space.

script   The written dialogue and instructions of a film, in written form.

sequence   A number of scenes grouped together in a particular order to tell a story.

shot   An image seen briefly on the screen, eg of a person laughing or a car pulling up.

social network (of Internet sites)   Putting information on the Internet for others.

special effects   Illusions in a film which aim to make the action more dramatic.

spectacle   An exciting public performance.

test screening   One of the first showings of a film to a chosen audience, to check whether any elements need to be changed at the last moment.

tsar   The emperor of Russia until the country became communist in 1917.

video   A method of capturing and displaying moving images without using film.

Further reading

Film studies (Teach Yourself) Warren Buckland (Hodder Headline, 1998)
Writing, Producing, and Directing Movies Geoffrey M. Horn (Gareth Stevens, 2006)
Film-making: All You Need to Know James Marsh (Hodder Children's Books, 1999)

Website links

Anim8ed
http://www.anim8ed.org.uk/

Blast film (BBC)
http://www.bbc.co.uk/blast/film/

Filmclub
http://www.filmclub.org/

Filmstreet
http://www.filmstreet.co.uk/default.aspa

Kids' Vid
http://kidsvid.altec.org/

Me and my movie (BBC)
http://www.bbc.co.uk/cbbc/meandmymovie/

Young film critic
http://www.youngfilmcritic.org/about.html

Index